The Ultimate Copywriting Guide: Transform Words into Sales

Nancy Rodriguez

Copyright © 2024

All rights reserved.

No part of this publication may be reproduced, distributed, or transmitted in any form or by any means, including photocopying, recording, or by any other electronic or mechanical process, except for brief citations in critical reviews and certain others, without prior consent. written. publisher permission non-commercial uses permitted by copyright law.

The Ultimate Copywriting Guide: Transform Words into Sales

Table of Contents

Introduction to Copywriting
-The Importance of Copywriting in Sales

1. Understanding Your Audience
   - Identifying Target Demographics
   - Creating Customer Personas

2. The Psychology of Persuasion
   - Key Principles of Persuasive Writing
   - How Emotions Drive Decisions

3. Crafting Compelling Headlines
   - Techniques for Hooking Your Readers
   - A/B Testing Headlines for Effectiveness

4. Structuring Your Copy
   - The Anatomy of Effective Copy
   - Using Clear and Engaging Formats

5. The Power of Storytelling
   - How Stories Create Connection
   - Crafting Narratives That Sell

6. Using Persuasive Techniques
   - Scarcity and Urgency
   - Social Proof and Testimonials

7. Writing for Different Mediums
   - Ad Copy vs. Website Copy vs. Email
   - Tailoring Your Message for Each Platform

8. Calls to Action That Convert
   - Designing Effective CTAs
   - Placement and Visibility Strategies

9. SEO and Copywriting
   - Integrating Keywords Naturally
   - Writing for Both Readers and Search Engines

10. Editing and Refining Your Copy
    - Tips for Polishing Your Writing
    - Common Mistakes to Avoid

11. Measuring Success
    - Key Metrics to Track
    - Analysing and Interpreting Data

12. Continuous Improvement
    - The Importance of Feedback
    - Iterating Based on Performance

13. Case Studies of Successful Copy
    - Analysing Effective Campaigns
    - Lessons Learned from Top Brands

14. Final Thoughts and Next Steps
    - Building a Copywriting Strategy
    - Resources for Further Learning

Introduction

Welcome to the world of copywriting. In this section, we'll look at what copywriting is and why it's important for sales. Understanding copywriting can help you communicate better and sell more efficiently, whether you are a business owner, marketer, or simply someone who enjoys writing.

What is copywriting?

Copywriting is the art of creating text that persuades people to take action. This can include purchasing a product, signing up for a newsletter, or clicking on a link. Unlike conventional writing, which may seek to inform or entertain, copywriting aims to persuade. It is about creating words that inspire readers to take action.

Think of copywriting as a link between your product and potential customers. Good writing is like a helpful guide, guiding them to a decision that benefits both sides. The better your writing, the more likely you are to close a transaction.

Why Is Copywriting Important in Sales?

1. First impressions matter.

When someone sees your advertisement or website, they build an opinion within seconds. Your copy is usually the first thing they see. If it's entertaining and straightforward, it'll get their attention immediately. If it is boring or perplexing, they may leave without exploring further. Good copywriting makes a good first impression, leaving readers wanting to learn more.

2. Establishing trust and credibility.

In a congested market, trust is critical. People are more likely to buy from brands that they recognise and trust. Well-written copy contributes to this trust. It can highlight your brand's personality and beliefs, allowing readers to feel engaged. Including testimonials and case studies in your content helps boost trust by demonstrating that genuine consumers have had great experiences with your product.

3. Emphasising benefits, not just features.

Many companies make the mistake of focussing solely on the characteristics of their products. While features are important, it is the benefits that customers value most. Good copywriting focuses on how a product can solve a problem or improve someone's life. Instead of saying, "This hoover has a powerful motor," you could say, "This hoover speeds up your cleaning, freeing up more time for the things you love."

4. Generating a sense of urgency

Copywriting can also convey a sense of urgency. When consumers believe they will lose out on a deal, they are more likely to act swiftly. Phrases such as "limited time offer" or "while supplies last" might prompt urgent action. This strategy can greatly increase sales, especially when combined with persuasive text.

5. Directing Action Through Calls to Action

A compelling call to action (CTA) is critical in copywriting. A CTA instructs readers on what to do next, whether it's "Buy Now," "Sign Up Today," or "Learn More." Effective CTAs are clear and persuasive, leading the reader to the intended action. They should elicit enthusiasm and a sense of urgency, making it simple for the reader to take the next action.

6. SEO and Online Visibility.

In today's digital age, successful copywriting entails understanding search engine optimization (SEO). Good writing will help your website rank higher in search engines, making it easier for potential clients to find you. By naturally including important keywords in your content, you can draw more visits to your site, boosting the likelihood of a sale.

7. Adapting to various formats.

Copywriting isn't one-size-fits-all. The style and tone of your writing can vary depending on where it appears. For example, social media posts, email newsletters, and site pages all have distinct formats and audiences. Understanding how to tailor your material to each platform is critical. Tailoring your message ensures that it resonates with your audience no matter where they see it.

8. Continuous improvement.

Copywriting is not a one-time activity. It necessitates constant testing and refinement. Analysing your copy's performance can reveal useful insights. Metrics such as click-through rates and conversion rates can reveal what works and what doesn't. You may boost the effectiveness of your copy over time by regularly refining it using real data.

Conclusion

Copywriting is a potent instrument that can help your sales efforts. Understanding its relevance will help you connect with your audience and persuade them to take action. Whether you're writing commercials, product descriptions, or website content, excellent copywriting may help.

As we progress through this tutorial, you will learn useful approaches and ideas for improving your copywriting talents. You'll learn how to create communications that resonate, generate trust, and ultimately increase revenue. Let us begin this adventure of transforming your words into powerful instruments for success!

One

Understanding Your Audience
Identifying Target Demographics
Creating Customer Personas

To excel at copywriting, you must first understand who you are writing for. This chapter will help you discover your target demographics and create consumer personas. Knowing your audience allows you to create messages that resonate and lead to increased sales.

Identifying target demographics.

What are demographics?

Demographics are the qualities that define a specific group of people. These may include age, gender, income, education level, geography, and others. Understanding these characteristics enables you to tailor your message to the needs of distinct groups.

Why demographics matter

Understanding your target demographics enables you to develop relevant content. For example, if you sell toys, your target audience is likely to be parents. If you're marketing a luxury car, your target audience could be rich folks. Each group has unique interests and demands, and your copy should reflect this.

How to Identify your target demographics

1. Research Existing Customers

Begin by looking at your current consumers. Who are they? What have they got in common? Analysing consumer data can reveal information about age, gender, geography, and shopping habits. This information is crucial for knowing your audience.

2. Use surveys and questionnaires.

Surveys are another means of gathering demographic information. Ask your consumers about their age, gender, interests, and purchasing habits. You can send surveys by email, social media, or your website. The responses will help you acquire a better understanding of your audience.

3. Analyse competitors.

Consider your competition and their customer base. Who is their target audience? What demographics are they focusing on? This analysis might show market gaps and assist you in identifying previously unknown target populations.

4. Use analytics tools.

If you have a website or social media presence, employ analytics tools to collect information. These tools can display the age, gender, location, and hobbies of your visitors. Platforms such as Google Analytics and Facebook Insights provide useful information that can help you with your marketing efforts.

Creating Customer Personas

After you've defined your target demographics, the following step is to develop consumer personas. A consumer persona is a thorough profile of the ideal customer. It extends beyond demographics to encompass behaviours, motivations, and obstacles.

Why Create Customer Personas?

Customer personas assist you envision your target audience. With a clear picture of who you're writing for, you may personalise your messaging to match their individual needs. This personalisation can increase engagement and conversion rates.

How to create customer personas

1. Gather data.

Begin by gathering data from your demographic research. Look for patterns and shared characteristics within your target audience. This will be the foundation for your consumer personas.

2. Identify goals and challenges.

Consider what goals your target audience wishes to attain. What issues do they have that your product or service can address? Understanding their motives and challenges can enable you to write more effectively. For example, if your target audience consists of busy parents, they may be looking for time-saving alternatives.

3. Create detailed profiles.

Once you have the information, make complete profiles for each persona. Add the following elements:

-Name: Give your persona a name so they feel more real.
- Demographics: Include your age, gender, income, and location.
- Background: Provide a brief description of their schooling and employment.
- Interests: - What activities do they enjoy in their free time?
- Goals: What do they want to achieve?
- Challenges: What obstacles do they face?

An example persona may look like this:

Name: Sarah, the Busy Mother
Demographics: Age 35, Female, Income $70,000. Live in the suburbs.
Background: College-educated; works part-time while raising two children.
Interests: Likes cooking, family activities, and exercise.
Goals: Wants to offer healthy meals for her family and save time.
Challenges: Struggling to combine job, family, and personal time.

4. Use personas in your copywriting.

Once you've identified your personalities, employ them to direct your writing. Consider the following questions: "What would Sarah think about this product?" or, "How can I address her challenges in my message?" Writing with your personas in mind will help your copy be more relatable and effective.

Conclusion

Understanding your target is the first step towards crafting a good copy. By defining target demographics and developing consumer profiles, you can create messages that will resonate with your audience. This understanding will result in stronger connections, increased engagement, and, eventually, higher sales. As you progress through this tutorial, keep your audience in mind and let their demands influence your writing. Your success will be determined by how well you understand and communicate with them.

Two

The Psychology of Persuasion Key Principles of Persuasive Writing How Emotions Drive Decisions

Understanding how people think and feel is essential for developing messages that persuade them to take action. We will talk about the main concepts of persuasive writing and how emotions influence decision-making.

Key Principles of Persuasive Writing

1. Know Your Audience

The first guideline of persuasive writing is to understand who you're talking to. This entails understanding their needs, desires, and pain spots. When you write with your audience in mind, you may develop messages that hit home. Use the client personas you created in the last chapter to inform your writing.

2. Use clear and simple language.

Effective persuasion necessitates clear communication. Avoid using jargon or sophisticated terminology that may confuse your readers. Instead, use straightforward language that is easy to comprehend. This makes your message more accessible and helps your audience get your argument quickly.

3. Establish credibility.

People are more willing to be convinced by someone they trust. To establish your credibility, provide evidence such as statistics, expert opinions, or testimonials. Sharing real-world client success stories can also help to establish trust. When your audience sees that others have had favourable experiences, they are more likely to trust your product or service.

4. Make a strong argument.

A convincing message should contain a clear argument. Begin with a great start that draws attention. Present your key claims coherently, supporting them with proof. Address any reservations your audience may have and offer counterarguments to comfort them. A well-structured argument can help readers reach your intended conclusion.

5. Use social proof.

Social evidence is a potent persuasion technique. It is based on the premise that people are impacted by the behaviours and beliefs of others. Using testimonials, case studies, and reviews can demonstrate to potential buyers that your product is trusted and valued. Highlighting the amount of delighted clients or positive reviews can help to promote this concept.

6. Appeal to Emotions.

Emotions play an important influence in decision making. When you connect emotionally with your audience, you have a better chance of persuading them. This takes us to the next part, which discusses how emotions influence decisions.

How Emotions Influence Decisions

The Role of Emotions

While people believe they make decisions based on rationality, emotions frequently guide their choices. Emotions can encourage people to take action, and understanding this can help you write better copy. Here are some important feelings to consider when writing.

1. Fear

Fear can be an effective motivator. It can motivate people to take action to avert an undesirable outcome. For example, if you're marketing home security systems, emphasising the potential of burglary might instil a sense of urgency. However, employ fear with caution. It should prompt action without overwhelming your viewers.

2. Trust

Trust is crucial in all relationships, including those between businesses and their customers. Building trust through open communication and credible information might result in increased conversion rates. Use testimonials and personal tales to help build trust.

3. Happiness.

People are frequently drawn to good emotions. When you can make your audience pleased or excited about a product, they are more likely to purchase. Use positive words and emphasise the benefits that can bring joy or happiness into their life.

4. Belongings have an innate need to belong to groups. You may use this by fostering a sense of community around your business. Use inclusive words to make your audience feel a part of something bigger. "Join the movement" or "Become a part of our family" are powerful phrases.

5. Anticipation

Anticipation can generate excitement for a product or service. Creating a feeling of what is to come might motivate people to act. For example, if you have a new product coming out soon, tease its features and benefits to generate interest. This can encourage your audience to stay tuned and take action once it becomes available.

Connecting Emotions with Copywriting

To effectively employ emotions in your writing, examine the following tips:

-Tell Stories: Stories can elicit emotions and make your message more relatable. Share personal anecdotes or client experiences that illustrate the emotions you wish to express. A good tale can help your audience feel more connected and understood.

-Use Vivid Language: Descriptive language helps create an image in the reader's head. Use phrases that conjure vivid images or experiences. This might elicit an emotional reaction and make your message more memorable.

-Focus on Benefits: When discussing your product, stress how it will benefit the customer's life. Rather than simply listing characteristics, emphasise the emotional benefits. Instead of saying, "This software saves time," you might say, "Picture having more time to enjoy with your family."

Create urgency: Use terms like "Limited time offer" or "Act now." This might generate a sense of urgency, encouraging readers to make a speedy decision.

Conclusion

Understanding the psychology of persuasion is critical for successful copywriting. You may create messages that resonate by understanding your target audience and utilising important persuasive writing techniques. Emotions play an important role in decision-making, so learn to appeal to them through your writing. As you begin to implement these ideas, you'll realise how efficiently your copy may persuade and engage your target audience, resulting in increased sales success.

Three

Crafting Compelling Headlines
Techniques for Hooking Your Readers
A/B Testing Headlines for Effectiveness

Headlines are the first thing your readers notice. A compelling headline can pique people's interest. In this chapter, we will look at ways for catching your viewers and the significance of A/B testing your headlines to determine what works best.

Techniques to Hook Your Readers

1. Use numbers.

Numbers may help your headline stand out. People enjoy lists because they provide quick and easy information. For example, "5 Tips for Better Sleep" sounds more appealing than "Tips for Better Sleep." Numbers provide a feeling of structure and a clear expectation of what readers will learn.

2. Ask questions.

Incorporating a question into your headline can pique readers' interest. For instance, For example, "Are you Committing These Common Copywriting Mistakes? " prompts readers to consider their own methods. Questions can captivate readers by prompting them to reflect on their own experiences and inspiring them to seek answers.

3. Generate a sense of urgency.

Use urgency in your headlines to encourage readers to act swiftly. Phrases like "Limited Time Offer" or "Don't Miss Out" instil anxiety of losing something precious. This sense of urgency can encourage readers to click through and discover more.

4. Use strong adjectives.

Using descriptive adjectives in your headline might improve its appeal. Instead of "Tips for Writing," use "Essential Tips for Writing Compelling Copy." Words like "essential," "incredible," or "ultimate" pique interest and make your information appear more valuable.

5. Make it Relatable

Headlines that tap into readers' emotions or experiences can be extremely successful. For example, "How to Overcome Writer's Block" addresses a prevalent problem. Relatable headlines demonstrate that you understand your audience's challenges and can provide solutions.

6. Use Powerful Words.

Power words are strong, descriptive words that elicit emotions. Words like "proven," "secret," "guaranteed," and "exclusive" can help make your headline more appealing. For example, "Discover the Secret to Successful Marketing" sounds more appealing than "Learn about Marketing."

7. Be clear and specific.

While creativity is valuable, clarity should never be sacrificed. A headline should state clearly what the piece is about. For example, "How to Write Great Copy" is straightforward and explains exactly what the reader will learn. Avoid ambiguous headlines that confuse readers.

8. Incorporate keywords.

Use relevant keywords in your headlines to boost your search engine rankings. This increases the likelihood that more people will discover your material. If your content is about "email marketing," using that phrase in the headline can help you reach the correct audience.

A/B Testing Headlines for Effectiveness.

After you've created numerous headline possibilities, the next step is to evaluate their effectiveness. A/B testing is a technique that involves comparing two variations of a headline to determine which one works better.

What is A/B testing?

A/B testing entails producing two distinct headlines for the same piece of content. You then present each headline to a segment of your audience. You can tell whether a headline is more effective by tracking how many clicks or engagements it receives.

Why is A/B Testing important?

A/B testing allows you to determine what resonates with your target audience. Sometimes the headline you believe is the best does not perform well. Testing enables you to make data-driven decisions, which improves your content strategy over time.

How to conduct A/B testing.

1. Choose Your Headlines: Begin with at least two headlines to test. Make sure they are sufficiently distinct to yield unambiguous results. For example, compare "10 Ways to Boost Your Productivity" versus "Increase Your Productivity with These 10 Tips."

2. Choose Your Audience: Determine which segments of your audience will see each headline. You can target email lists, social media following, or website visits. To obtain trustworthy findings, ensure that the groups are roughly the same size.

3. Establish a Timeframe: Determine how long you will run the test. This could take a few days or a week, depending on the size of your audience and amount of interaction. Allow adequate time for the data to be collected.

4. Analyse the Results: After the testing time, compare the performance of the headlines. Consider KPIs such as click-through rate, engagement, and conversions. Determine which headline fared better, and why.

5. Use the Winning title: Once you've determined the most effective title, incorporate it into your content. This will boost your chances of acquiring new readers and meeting your objectives.

Tips for A/B testing headlines

Test One Variable at a Time: For clear results, only change one part of the headline at a time. This could be to the wording, the use of figures, or the emotional appeal. Testing numerous variables at once can produce ambiguous findings.

-Keep It Simple: For testing, use plain, uncomplicated headlines. Complex or too inventive headlines might skew results, making it difficult to discern which works.

-Monitor Performance Over Time: A/B testing is not a one-time activity. To optimise your results, test headlines for various types of content on a regular basis.

Conclusion

Creating intriguing headlines is critical for capturing your readers' attention. You can use strategies such as figures, questions, and related language to generate headlines that intrigue and engage readers. A/B testing helps you to modify your headlines using real data, ensuring that your content reaches the intended audience. With practice, you'll become adept at crafting headlines that not only entice clicks but also inspire real engagement.

Four

Structuring Your Copy
The Anatomy of Effective Copy
Using Clear and Engaging Formats

The Anatomy of Effective Copy

1. Headline

The headline is the initial element that captures readers' attention.
It must capture the reader's attention and entice them to continue reading. A good title should be straightforward, entertaining, and related to the content. Make your headline stand out by using strategies such as numbers, questions, or powerful words.

2) Subheadings

Subheadings separate the text and make it easier to scan. They direct readers through your material, emphasising important aspects. Use subheadings to separate your material into sections. This not only enhances readability, but also allows readers to discover the information they seek more quickly.

3. Introduction.

The introduction establishes the context for your message. It should entice readers and explain what they can expect. To capture their attention, begin with a fascinating remark or question. Clearly define the aim of your work and the rewards that the reader will receive.

4. Body

The body is where you'll deliver your primary thoughts. Each paragraph should concentrate on a single point to make your writing clean and organised. Use brief paragraphs that are easy to understand. This helps to keep readers interested and avoids overwhelming them with too much information at once.

5. Use of bullets and lists.

Bulleted lists and numbered points can help your writing become more interesting. They break up large chunks of text and highlight key information. Lists are simple to peruse, helping readers to swiftly grasp important insights. For example, if you're offering advice, arrange it as a list to improve clarity.

6. Call to action (CTA).

Every piece of text should have a clear call to action. A CTA encourages readers to take the next step, such as signing up for a newsletter, making a purchase, or contacting you. Use action-oriented wording and ensure that your CTA sticks out. Phrases like "Get Started Today" and "Join Now" can be quite powerful.

7. Conclusion.

The conclusion summarises your message. It should summarise the main aspects and emphasise the benefits. A good ending can also reinforce the call to action, prompting readers to take the desired action. To keep them interested, leave them with one final thought or inquiry.

Using clear and engaging formats.

1. Select the appropriate format for your audience.

varied formats elicit varied responses from audiences. Understand your readers and their preferences. For example, a younger audience may favour brief, visually appealing information such as infographics, whereas a professional audience may prefer extensive reports or articles.

2. Use visuals.

Incorporating visuals can improve engagement. Images, graphs, and charts can help break up text and illustrate your points more effectively. Visuals make your text more engaging and understandable. Make sure any visuals you utilise are related to your message.

3. Keep it Scannable.

Many readers skim the information instead of reading every word. To accommodate this, employ scanning-friendly formatting strategies. Use brief paragraphs, bold language for emphasis, and a lot of white space. This guides the reader's eye and allows them to rapidly identify crucial information.

4. Maintain a consistent style.

Using a consistent style across your material creates a more unified reading experience. This involves using a consistent font, colour scheme, and tone. A consistent style makes your material appear professional and credible. It also strengthens your brand's identity.

5. Optimise for Mobile.

More individuals are viewing material on their mobile devices than ever before. Make your material easy to read on smaller displays. Use larger letter sizes, shorter paragraphs, and plenty of white space. Test your content on a variety of devices to ensure it looks excellent and is easy to browse.

6. Add Hyperlinks.

If your copy is online, include hyperlinks to provide extra information. This helps readers to delve deeper into issues without detracting from your primary material. Make sure the links are relevant and point to high-quality sources. However, don't overwhelm your material with links, as this might be distracting.

7. Edit and revise

After you've finished writing your copy, spend some time editing and revising it. Look for opportunities to increase clarity and flow. Check for grammar mistakes and odd language. A well-edited piece is more professional and easier for readers to understand.

8. Use Feedback.

Consider soliciting comments from others before releasing your copy. Fresh eyes can spot issues you may have overlooked and provide vital feedback on how your content reads. Use their input to improve your copy even further.

Conclusion

Structuring your material correctly is critical for engaging your readers. By focussing on crucial aspects such as headlines, subheadings, and clear formatting, you can generate material that is simple to read and understand. Use images, stick to a consistent design, and optimise for mobile to improve the user experience. With careful organisation and attention to detail, your text will not only inform but also motivate readers to take action.

Five

The Power of Storytelling
How Stories Create Connection
Crafting Narratives That Sell

Stories have a special potential to connect with people. They evoke emotions, form ties, and make concepts remember. In this chapter, we'll look at how tales form connections and how to write narratives that sell.

How Stories Create Connections

1. Emotional engagement
Stories evoke our emotions. They have the power to stir emotions like joy, sorrow, excitement, or fear. When we connect emotionally, we are more likely to recall and apply the message. For example, a tale about overcoming obstacles can motivate and make readers feel understood. This emotional connection is quite effective in establishing trust with your audience.

2. Relatability

People identify with stories that match their own experiences. When readers see themselves in a story, they form a link. For example, if you tell a personal tale about a professional problem, others may be able to relate. This relatability strengthens your message and motivates people to interact with your content.

3. Simplifying complex ideas.

Stories can help to simplify complicated subjects. Instead of delivering dry data, a tale can help to illustrate concepts in an understandable manner. For example, telling a story about a customer's journey can help clarify how your solution addresses an issue. This makes the content more approachable and relatable, allowing readers to understand the message

without becoming overwhelmed.

4. Memorable messaging.

People retain stories better than facts or data. A compelling story remains in the mind long after it is heard or read. When you incorporate your message into a tale, it becomes more memorable. For example, telling a story about how your product transformed someone's life would have a greater impact than simply listing features.

5. Building Trust

Sharing genuine experiences helps to establish trust with your audience. Transparency promotes credibility. When you describe your path, including both accomplishments and disappointments, readers see you as a real person rather than a brand. This genuineness builds loyalty and encourages readers to support your company.

Crafting Narratives that Sell

1. Know Your Audience

Understand your target audience before you begin writing your story. What are their interests, difficulties, and values?

Customise your story to resonate with them. For example, if your target audience is young professionals, offer stories that represent their experiences and goals.

2. Identify the core message.

Every story should carry a clear message. What do you hope your audience will take away? Whether it's the advantages of your product or the significance of a specific concept, make sure your primary message is woven throughout the story. This guarantees that readers comprehend the point of your article.

3. Create a relatable protagonist.

A compelling protagonist is essential to your plot. This persona should be relatable and reflect the audience's challenges or desires. Readers will relate more intimately if they recognise themselves in the protagonist's path. For example, if you're selling fitness products, your protagonist could be someone who struggles with motivation but eventually achieves their objectives.

4. Use Conflict and Resolution.

Every excellent story contains strife. This clash heightens suspense and keeps readers engaged. It could be an impediment that the protagonist faces, such as self-doubt or outside challenges. The resolution should demonstrate how the protagonist resolves the dilemma, frequently with the assistance of your product or service. This framework not only keeps readers interested, but it also emphasises the importance of what you're presenting.

5. Include sensory details.

Sensory elements make your story come to life. Utilize rich, descriptive language that stimulates the senses of sight, sound, taste, touch, and smell, helping readers dive deep into the story. Instead of expressing "The café was busy," you could say "The café buzzed with laughter, and the aroma of freshly brewed coffee filled the air." The use of vivid imagery adds to the story's appeal.

6. Keep it concise.

Stories are powerful, but they should also be brief. Avoid superfluous information that may detract from the essential point. Maintain narrative focus and ensure that each element has a purpose. A well-structured story is easier for readers to understand and remember.

7. Close with a powerful call to action.

Your story should culminate in a clear call to action. After sharing your story, tell readers what to do next. Make it obvious what the next steps are, whether they are visiting your website, signing up for a subscription, or making a purchase. A compelling CTA maintains the connection established by the story and encourages action.

8. Test and refine your stories.

After you've finished writing your story, run it with your intended audience. Gather feedback to determine what resonates and what does not. Use this input to improve your tale even further. A/B testing multiple versions of your narrative can help you figure out which components are most effective in increasing engagement and sales

Conclusion

Storytelling is a strong technique for building relationships and increasing revenue. Stories may make your message more memorable by activating emotions, clarifying complicated ideas, and fostering trust. Knowing your audience, generating sympathetic characters, and skilfully utilising conflict and resolution are all necessary for crafting sellable storylines. Your stories can encourage readers to take meaningful action by using sensory elements and a clear call to action. Accept the power of storytelling and see how it improves your text and engages your audience.

Six

Using Persuasive Techniques
Scarcity and Urgency
Social Proof and Testimonials

Persuasion is crucial in copywriting. It assists you in persuading readers to take action, whether it's completing a purchase, signing up for a subscription, or engaging with your business.

Scarcity and urgency

1. Understanding scarcity.

Scarcity denotes the finite availability of a product or service.

When people perceive something is in low supply, they desire it even more. The prospect of missing out might motivate action. For instance, you could say, "Just 5 remaining!"

It conveys a sense of urgency. People don't want to pass up the opportunity to acquire.

2. Creating urgency

Urgency takes the shortage one step further. It motivates people to act rapidly. Phrases such as "Limited time offer" or "Sale ends at midnight" promote quick action. When readers fear they will lose out, they are more likely to make a decision straight away.

3. Applying Time Limits

Setting a time constraint is a good method to generate urgency. For example, if you offer a discount that is only valid for 24 hours, readers will feel compelled to act quickly. Clear deadlines encourage people to make speedier decisions. Use countdown clocks on your website to highlight the urgency.

4. Examples of scarcity and urgency

Consider an online store with a promotion in which the first 100 customers receive a special discount. You can say, "Hurry! Only a few spots remain!" This stresses both shortage and urgency. The combination motivates customers to act before it's too late.

5. Ethical considerations

While scarcity and urgency are effective tools, they must be used appropriately. Avoid exaggerating or creating a false shortage. Customers who believe they are being manipulated may lose trust. Always make sure that your statements are accurate and reflect the real availability of your items or services.

Social proof and testimonials.

1. What is Social Proof?

The concept of social proof holds that people base their own actions and ideas on those of others. If a large number of individuals buy something or say positive things about it, others are more likely to do the same. Social proof promotes trust and trustworthiness.

2. Types of Social Proof

You can utilise a variety of social proofs:

-Customer Reviews: Positive feedback from customers can enhance trust in your product. Including star ratings or personal testimonials can make a significant impact.

-**Case Studies:** Detailed case studies demonstrate how your product has benefited others. They provide real-world instances that potential clients can relate to.

-**User-Generated Content:** Encourage customers to share their experiences via social media. Reposting their material demonstrates that actual people like and trust your company.

-**Influencer Endorsements:** Collaborating with influencers can help boost reputation. When a trustworthy figure recommends your product, their followers are more likely to consider it.

3. Creating Effective Testimonials

Testimonials are a strong source of social proof. Here's how you can make the most of them.

-**Be particular:** Instead of making general assertions, ask customers to discuss particular benefits. A testimonial like "This product saved me 10 hours a week!" has more impact than "It's great!"

-**Use Real Names and Photos:** When possible, provide the customer's name and a photo. This adds authenticity and helps the testimonial seem more trustworthy.

-**Highlight Results:** Emphasise the benefits your product brings. Demonstrate how it resolves an issue or enhances the customer's life.

4. Displaying Testimonials.

Make sure to include testimonials prominently on your website. Place them on product pages, landing pages, or your website's homepage. Consider building a dedicated testimonials page so potential customers can learn about other people's experiences.

5. Leveraging Case Studies

Case studies can be especially useful in B2B marketing. They provide a detailed insight at how your product has helped a client. Structure your case study to cover the problem, solution, and outcomes. This not only conveys a tale, but also exhibits genuine worth.

6. Encourage Reviews

Encourage satisfied consumers to submit feedback. You can send follow-up emails following a purchase or make a request on your website. Make things easier for them by including links to review platforms.
Provide incentives, like discounts on future purchases, to motivate more reviews.

7. Responding to Feedback.

Engage with customers who write both positive and negative reviews. Thank people who provide favourable comments, and resolve any problems raised in negative evaluations. This demonstrates to potential clients that you value their experience and are devoted to continuous development.

Conclusion

Scarcity, urgency, social proof, and testimonials are all effective persuasive methods that can improve your copy. Scarcity and urgency encourage fast action, whereas social proof fosters trust and credibility. Understanding and executing these tactics will increase engagement and motivate your audience to take significant action. Remember to apply these methods ethically to build trust and long-term connections with your customers.

Seven

Writing for Different Mediums Ad Copy vs. Website Copy vs. Email Tailoring Your Message for Each Platform

Marketing writing varies tremendously depending on the medium. Each platform has a distinct style and purpose. Understanding these distinctions is critical for effectively reaching and engaging your audience. Let's take a look at ad copy, website copy, and email, and how to customise your message to each.

Comparing ad copy, website copy, and email

1. Advertising Copy

Ad copy is concise and focused. Its primary purpose is to capture attention rapidly. Whether for social media, print advertisements, or web banners, ad copy must be concise and engaging.

Brevity is essential: You typically only have a few seconds to pique someone's curiosity. Use bold, straightforward language. A strong headline can have a major impact.

For example, "Get 50% Off Today Only!" notifies the reader right away what they'll benefit from.

-Call to Action (CTA): An effective CTA is necessary. Inform the reader exactly what to do next, such as "Shop Now" or "Sign Up Today." Make it easy for them to act.

-Emotional Appeal: Advertisements frequently exploit emotional impulses. Whether it's happiness, terror, or nostalgia, triggering an emotion might elicit a stronger reaction. Use pictures and language that will connect with your readers.

2. Web copy

The website copy is more descriptive and informative. It conveys critical information about your company, products, or services. Unlike advertisements, it provides for more detailed explanations

-Clarity and Structure: The website copy should be straightforward and well-organised. To improve readability, use headings, bullet points, and short paragraphs. Visitors frequently skim content, so make it clear.

-SEO Considerations: Include keywords relevant to your business. This improves your site's ranking in search engines, making it easier for potential customers to locate you. Incorporate these terms naturally within the content.

-Value : Clearly define what distinguishes you. Address the question: "What makes you the best choice?"Highlight your distinct advantages and solutions.

-Increase engagement by encouraging interaction. Include links to blog posts, FAQs, and contact forms. This keeps visitors interested and gives them more options to interact with your brand.

3. E-mail Copy

Email copy is personalised and straightforward. It frequently targets specific sections of your audience. The idea is to create relationships and increase conversions.

-Personalisation: Include the recipient's name and adapt the material to their preferences. Personalised emails outperform generic ones. For example, "Hi Sarah, these products are perfect for you!" seems more appealing.

-topic Lines: The topic line is important. It determines whether an email is opened. Keep it succinct yet obvious. Phrases like "Exclusive Offer Just for You!" can encourage readers to click.

-Value and Relevance: Offer valuable stuff. This could include exclusive discounts, helpful suggestions, or updates. Ensure that it is relevant to the reader's requirements and interests.

-Clear CTA: Like ad copy, emails require a clear call to action. Tell the reader what to do next, whether it's visiting your website, signing up for an event, or making a purchase.

Tailoring Your Message to Each Platform

1. Know Your Audience

Understanding your target is essential for adapting your message. Different platforms target different demographics. Understand who you're writing for and what they anticipate from each media.

-**Ad Copy:** Use emotional triggers that resonate fast. Keep it light-hearted and appealing.

-**Website Copy:** Provide detailed information to build trust. Your audience may be looking for information before making a decision.

-**Email:** Understand the inclinations of your audience segments. Customise your messages depending on previous interactions or purchases.

2. Adjust Your Tone.

The tone of your writing should correspond to the platform.

-**Ad Copy:** Use a bright, dynamic tone. It should be exciting and appealing.

-**Website Copy:** A professional and informed tone is preferred. It should appear authoritative while staying friendly.

-When sending emails, maintain a polite and conversational tone. This creates a sense of connection with the reader.

3. Format and Length

Each medium has different formatting requirements.

-Ad copy: Keep it short and sweet. Use compelling language and imagery.

-The website copy is longer and more structured. Use headings, bullet points, and illustrations to break up the content.

-Email: Moderate length. Get to the point while providing enough detail to inform and engage.

4. Testing and Optimisation

Don't be afraid to try alternative ways. What works for one audience may not work for others. Track the performance of your content across several platforms.

-Conduct A/B testing with alternative headlines, CTAs, and layouts. Determine which versions perform best.

-input: Get input from your audience. This can reveal insights into what resonates and what does not.

5. Consistency across platforms.

While the message should be adjusted to each channel, consistency is essential. Your brand voice and key message should remain consistent. This increases recognition and trust.

-Brand Voice: Whether it's funny or serious, maintain a consistent voice across all channels.

-Core Message: Make sure your brand's key idea is obvious whenever the audience encounters it.

Conclusion

Writing for various mediums necessitates an awareness of each platform's distinct features. Ad text should be eye-catching and concise, website copy should be educational and structured, and email writing should be personalised and engaging. By adapting your message to each channel, you can effectively connect with your audience and motivate them to act. Accept these distinctions, and your marketing efforts will provide better results.

Eight

Calls to Action That Convert
- Designing Effective CTAs
- Placement and Visibility Strategies

Calls to action (CTAs) are essential for moving your audience to the next step. A well-designed CTA may greatly increase conversions, whether they are making a purchase, subscribing to a newsletter, or downloading a resource. Let's look at how to construct effective CTAs and where to place them for the most visibility.

Designing Effective CTAs

1. Use clear and direct language.

Your call to action must employ clear and direct language. Avoid ambiguous wording. Instead of "Click here," use more specific commands such as "Get Your Free Guide" or "Start Your Free Trial." This explains exactly what the reader should expect.

2. Use action-oriented verbs.

Begin your CTAs with strong action verbs. Words like "Get," "Download," "Join," or "Shop" instil a sense of urgency and encourage instant action. For instance, "Download Now" is more enticing than just "Download."

3. Generate a sense of urgency.

Urgency can lead to quicker decisions. Phrases such as "Limited Time Offer" or "Only a Few Left!" make readers believe they will miss out if they do not act quickly. This may encourage them to click on your CTA without hesitation.

4. Highlight the benefits.

Make sure your CTA communicates the importance of taking action. Instead of simply describing what they will do, explain what is in it for them. For example, "Get Your Free Trial and Save 20%" emphasises both action and benefit.

5. Keep it short.

CTAs should be brief. Ideally, they should be kept to a few words. A simple message is easier to comprehend and recall. Aim for clarity while not overpowering the reader.

6. Design Matters

The design of your CTA is equally crucial as the message. Use hues that contrast with the rest of the page. The button should be visually appealing and noticeable, but not so enormous that it appears obtrusive.

7. Use first-person language.

Using first-person phrasing might make the CTA feel more personalised. Phrases such as "Start My Free Trial" or "Get My Discount" can help you connect with the reader. It helps individuals feel as if the action is personally relevant to them.

Placement and Visibility Strategy

1. Above the fold.

Position your CTAs above the fold, which means they should be visible without scrolling. Most visitors will glance here first, so make your major CTAs easy to spot right away.

2. Strategic placement.

Consider the flow of your text. CTAs should be put where they are contextually appropriate. For example, following a great blog post, a CTA for a similar resource or service may feel natural.

3. Repetition.

Don't be hesitant to include CTAs throughout your text. This enhances the likelihood that readers will encounter and interact with them. Simply ensure that each instance is appropriate and not excessively repetitious.

4. Use Visual cues.

Visual cues can help direct the reader's attention to your CTA. Arrows, images, or even surrounding white space can catch the eye. If your CTA is surrounded by empty space, it will stand out more.

5. Calls to Action at the End of Content

Insert CTAs at the conclusion of your material, such as blog entries or articles. After reading your material, readers may be more motivated to take action. A suggestion like "Are you ready to learn more?" Signing up for our newsletter can be effective.

6. In-line CTAs

Consider including in-line CTAs in your text. For example, if you describe a product or service, put a link or button directly there. This can pique people's curiosity at precisely the right time.

7. Mobile Optimisation.

Ensure that your CTAs are mobile-friendly. Many users access content through mobile phones, so make sure the buttons are easy to click and readable on smaller screens. Test your CTAs on a variety of devices to verify they work properly everywhere.

8. Testing and Analysis

Always test many variations of your CTAs. Use A/B testing to determine which wording, design, and location produce the best results. Monitor analytics to determine how well your CTAs are performing and make changes as needed.

9. Address the User Intent.

Understanding your audience's preferences can help you create effective CTAs. If a visitor is reading about a problem, provide a solution that is directly tied to the issue. For example, if they're reading about healthy eating, a call to action for a meal planning guide would be appropriate.

10. Use social proof.

Social proof can help improve your CTAs. If possible, show how many people have already joined up or downloaded something. Phrases like "Join 1,000+ Happy Customers" can boost confidence and inspire action.

Conclusion

Calls to action are essential for converting website visitors into consumers. You may direct your audience's actions by creating powerful CTAs that use clear language, strong verbs, and noticeable placement. Consider the flow of your content, incorporate urgency and benefits, and always test your tactics. With the correct CTAs in place, you can drastically increase conversion rates and expand your business.

Nine

SEO and Copywriting Integrating Keywords Naturally Writing for Both Readers and Search Engines

SEO, or search engine optimization, is critical for promoting your material online. Good copywriting and good SEO methods can help your website rank better in search results. This chapter discusses how to naturally integrate keywords and write for both readers and search engines.

Integrating Keywords Naturally

1. Understanding Keywords.

Keywords are the words and phrases that users enter into search engines when looking for information. Selecting the appropriate keywords is the first stage in SEO. Use Google Keyword Planner or Ubersuggest to find keywords related to your topic. Look for keywords with an appropriate balance of search traffic and competition.

2. Placement of keywords

Once you've identified your keywords, it's critical to use them strategically into your content:

-Title: Include the main term in the title. This allows search engines to better understand your material.

-Include keywords in headings and subheadings. This not only improves SEO, but also makes your text easier to read.

In the first 100 words of your introduction, include your primary keyword. This indicates to search engines that your information is relevant.

-Throughout the Content: Use keywords naturally throughout your article. Avoid keyword stuffing, which involves pushing too many keywords into your content. This can make your content sound odd and result in penalties from search engines.

3. Synonyms and related phrases.

Using synonyms and similar phrases might help your SEO without making your content appear forced. Search engines are intelligent enough to recognise variants on terms. For example, if your primary keyword is "dog training," you may include "pet training," "obedience training," or "canine training." This variation makes your writing more natural and intriguing.

4. Optimise Meta Tags.

Meta tags are short text descriptions that summarise the content of a page. They do not appear on the page, but rather in the HTML code. Make sure to include your core keyword in both the meta title and meta description. This assists search engines in interpreting your content and improves click-through rates.

5. Image Alt Text.

If you utilise photos in your material, add keywords in the alt text. This allows search engines to index your photographs and enhances accessibility for visually impaired users. For example, if you have a photo of a dog training session, add the alt text "dog training session with a golden retriever."

Write for both readers and search engines.

1. Concentrate on quality content.

First and foremost, your content should be useful to readers. High-quality content engages visitors and encourages them to share it. If your writing lacks meaningful information, no amount of SEO will help.

2. Know Your Audience

Understanding your audience is essential. Write in a way that addresses their interests and needs. Use a tone and style that speaks to them. This not only boosts engagement, but also increases the possibility that people will share your material.

3. Balance readability and SEO.

Your writing should be simple to read. Use brief paragraphs, bullet points, and straightforward language. If your writing is dense and difficult to grasp, readers may quit immediately. Keep phrases simple and to the point. Aim for a conversational tone that will draw readers in.

4. Encourage engagement.

Include questions and suggestions that will inspire readers to interact with your content. For example, ask for their ideas or experiences with your topic. This not only enhances the user experience, but it also increases the amount of time they spend on your page, which can benefit SEO.

5. Internal and External Links.

Linking to other relevant information can help improve both readability and SEO. Internal links direct viewers to different pages on your website, keeping them interested longer. External links to credible sites can boost the trustworthiness of your article. Simply make sure that the connections are relevant and valuable to your viewers.

6. Use structured data.

Structured data allows search engines to better understand your material. It increases your chances of appearing in rich snippets, which are enhanced search results. Use schema markup to add context to your content, such as product details, reviews, or articles.

7. Monitor analytics.

Keep an eye on your website's metrics. Tools such as Google Analytics can show you how well your material is performing. Analyse indicators such as page views, bounce rate, and average time on page. This data can assist you determine what works and what needs to be improved.

8. Stay current on SEO trends.

SEO is constantly changing. Stay up to date on the most recent trends and modifications to search algorithms. Follow credible SEO sites and forums to keep your knowledge up to date. Adapting to change can provide you an advantage over competition.

9. Create Engaging Headlines.

Your headlines are the first thing people see, so make them memorable and informative. Include keywords while keeping them appealing. For example, instead of "Dog Training Tips," try "10 Essential Tips for Successful Dog Training." This not only contains a term, but also entices the reader.

10. Be patient.

SEO takes time. Do not anticipate instant results. It may take weeks or even months to notice substantial changes in your rankings. Focus on developing high-quality content and improving your SEO methods, and you should see favourable results in the long run.

Conclusion

Integrating SEO into your copywriting is critical for reaching a wider audience. Use keywords naturally, create high-quality material, and write with both readers and search engines in mind. By harmonising these components, you may develop captivating content that ranks well and engages your target audience. Remember that the idea is to add value while making your information discoverable. With patience and practice, you can learn the art of SEO and copywriting.

Ten

Editing and Refining Your Copy
Tips for Polishing Your Writing
Common Mistakes to Avoid

Editing plays a key role in the writing process. It allows you to refine your work, ensuring clarity and effectiveness. This chapter offers suggestions for improving your writing and identifies typical errors to avoid.

Tips for improving your writing

1. Take A Break

Take a break when you've finished your first draft. This respite helps you to return with a fresh perspective. You will be better equipped to identify mistakes and places for improvement. Even a couple of hours can make a difference.

2. Read aloud.

Reading your material aloud allows you to identify uncomfortable words and typos that you would overlook when reading silently. It lets you hear how your sentences flow. If something sounds off, it usually has to be reworked.

3. Check for Clarity.

Ensure that your thoughts are clear. If a sentence is ambiguous, reword it. Consider whether a reader who is inexperienced with the topic will understand your message. Aim for simplicity and directness.

4. Concentrate on Structure.

Ensure that your information follows a logical structure. Each paragraph should have a distinct main theme, and transitions between them should be seamless. Headings and subheadings can help readers navigate your material by breaking up the text.

5. Remove unnecessary words.

Be brutal with your editing. Remove any words or phrases that don't add value to the message. Aim for brevity. For example, instead of stating "due to the fact that," use "Because." This strengthens your writing.

6. Vary your sentence length.

Using a combination of short and large sentences makes your writing more engaging. Short sentences can make an effect, yet lengthier ones can convey detail. A nice rhythm helps keep the reader interested.

7. Check for consistency.

Consistency in tone, style, and formatting is necessary. Ensure that you use the same voice throughout your piece. If you start with a formal tone, don't change it halfway through. Also, make sure that your formatting (such as bullet points or numbering) is consistent.

8. Use an active voice.

The active voice makes your writing clearer and more lively. Instead of stating "The book was read by John," say "John read the book." This ensures that your writing remains engaging and clear.

9. Seek feedback

Share your work with others to gather feedback. A fresh perspective can bring to light concerns that you may have ignored. To get the finest insights, choose someone who is knowledgeable with your audience or topic matter.

10. Proofread carefully.

Proofreading is the last stage. Check for spelling, grammatical, and punctuation mistakes. Use programs like Grammarly or Hemingway to detect errors, but don't rely entirely on them. Always conduct your own job review.

Common Mistakes To Avoid

1. Overuse of Jargon.

Using excessive technical language or jargon may alienate your audience. If your audience is unfamiliar with certain phrases, clarify them or use simpler language. Aim for language that everyone understands.

2. Ignore Your Audience

Always keep your intended audience in mind. Write in a way that addresses their needs and interests. Failure to regard your readers can result in unsatisfactory material.

3. Lack of focus

Stay on topic. Avoid straying into unrelated topics that can dilute your message. Each paragraph should support your main point. If you find yourself wandering off on a tangent, consider creating a new section or removing the text altogether.

4. Neglecting Visual Elements

Visual aids, such as images or charts, can improve comprehension. If your post is entirely text-heavy, consider using pictures to break it up. This can improve your content's engagement and digestibility.

5. Not using subheadings

Subheadings help to structure your information and direct readers. Without them, your text may feel overwhelming. To boost readability, organise your content into parts with clear headings.

6. Failure to Edit Thoroughly

Do not rush the editing process. Skimming over your work can result in undetected errors. Take the time to properly review your writing. Multiple rounds of editing might result in a more polished finished product.

7. Ignoring formatting.

Formatting can influence how your material is perceived. Maintain consistency in fonts, sizes, and styles. Pay care to line spacing and margins. A well-formatted document is more appealing and simple to read.

8. Being overly attached.

Sometimes authors become overly wedded to their words. Be willing to remove or change sections of your writing that do not contribute to the overall message. It's about the material, not your personal connection to it.

9. Using Spell Check Alone

Spell Check can detect many problems, but it is not flawless. It may not detect homophones (such as "there" vs. "their") or context-specific errors. Always proofread your work personally to ensure a comprehensive assessment.

10. Disregarding the Call to Action

If your writing is intended to inspire certain action, remember to add a strong call to action. Whether it's signing up for a subscription or completing a purchase, tell your reader what to do next.

Conclusion

Editing and improving your material is critical to producing clear, effective writing. By following these guidelines and avoiding frequent blunders, you can considerably improve your work. Remember that the goal is to communicate clearly and engage your audience. Take the time to improve your writing; the outcome will speak for themselves.

Eleven

Measuring Success
Key Metrics to Track
Analysing and Interpreting Data

Measuring the success of your text is critical for understanding its impact and optimising future efforts. Knowing which metrics to track and how to interpret the data will allow you to make more informed decisions. This chapter discusses critical metrics to monitor and how to interpret the findings effectively.

Key Metrics To Track

1. Conversion Rate.
The conversion rate indicates how many visitors complete a desired action, such as making a purchase or subscribing to a newsletter. Divide the number of conversions by the total number of visitors and then multiply the result by 100. For example, if 50% of 1,000 visitors made a purchase, your conversion rate would be 5%. A greater conversion rate denotes effective copywriting.

2. Clickthrough Rate (CTR)

CTR measures how many people clicked on a link versus how many viewed it. It's very critical for email and advertising. To calculate CTR, divide the number of clicks by the number of impressions (views), then multiply by 100. For example, if your ad generated 200 clicks out of 10,000 impressions, your CTR would be 2%. A higher CTR indicates that your headlines and call to actions are intriguing.

3. Bounce Rate

The bounce rate is the percentage of visitors who abandon your website after just seeing one page. A high bounce rate could indicate that your content is neither interesting or relevant to visitors. To calculate it, divide the number of single-page views by the total number of visitors to your website. For example, if 300 of 1,000 visitors leave after viewing one page, your bounce rate is 30%. Aim for a reduced bounce rate to indicate that visitors are researching your website deeper.

4. Average Time on Page.
This measure indicates the average length of time visitors spend on a certain page. A longer average time indicates that your material is compelling and maintains reader interest. To determine this, divide the total time spent on a page by the number of visits. If people spend several minutes reading your content, it's a solid indication that your writing speaks to them.

Return on Investment (ROI)

ROI determines the profitability of your copywriting efforts. To determine ROI, remove your marketing costs from the income generated, divide by the cost, and multiply by 100. For example, if you invested $1,000 in a campaign and made $5,000 in sales, your ROI is 400%. A positive ROI indicates that your text is effective at generating revenue.

6. Engagement Metrics.

Likes, shares, comments, and other social media or website interactions are all considered engagement indicators. High engagement implies that your audience values your material. Keep an eye on these indicators to see what your readers are responding to. If a piece receives a lot of shares, try publishing similar material in the future.

7. Lead Generation

If your goal is to produce leads, keep track of how many leads you capture with your copy. This could involve newsletter subscriptions, free trials, and downloads. Compare the amount of leads generated to your total traffic to determine how effective your material is at drawing new consumers.

Analyse and interpret data.

1. Setting Goals.

Set clear goals for your copy. Having precise goals, whether it is to increase sales, attract more subscribers, or raise brand awareness, will help lead your analysis.

2. Use analytics tools.

Google Analytics, social media insights, and email marketing dashboards all provide useful data. Familiarise yourself with these tools for monitoring your critical metrics. They can help you see trends and patterns in your data, making it easier to analyse the results.

3. Evaluate performance throughout time.

Analyse your stats over time to detect trends. Is your conversion rate improving? Is your bounce rate decreasing? Comparing data from different time periods can help you determine the effectiveness of your improvements. For example, if you updated your landing page, see whether there was a noticeable boost in conversions.

4. Segment your audience.

Segmenting your audience helps you to analyse data for certain groups. This could be based on demographics, behaviour, or the source of traffic. Understanding how different groups respond to your material allows you to modify your messages more successfully. For example, if younger viewers prefer certain types of material, create more of those.

5. Identify high-performing content.

Look patterns in your top-performing content. What themes, headlines, or styles are most popular with your audience? Identifying these patterns can help you plan your future writing. If blog posts containing lists receive greater traffic, consider writing more list-based articles.

6. Experiment and A/B Test.

Testing multiple versions of your material can reveal what works best. A/B testing entails developing two different versions of your content and comparing their performance. For example, you may test two different titles to determine which one gets more hits. Use the results to improve your technique based on actual facts.

7. Learn from failures.

Not all content will perform well, and that's fine. Determine what went wrong with the underperforming items. Was the message unclear? Did it fail to engage the audience? Learning from your failures is critical to enhancing your future performance.

8. Keep track of competitors.

Monitor your competitors to learn about their techniques. Which metrics are they focussing on? How do their engagement levels compare with yours? This might help you understand industry trends and find opportunities for development.

9. Regularly review and adjust.

Make data analysis a frequent component of your workflow. Set aside time each month or quarter to monitor your stats and evaluate your copy's performance. Use this opportunity to adapt your plans based on what the data shows.

10. Celebrate Successes

Finally, do not forget to congratulate your accomplishments. When your KPIs demonstrate improvement, acknowledge the effort that went into it. Celebrating modest victories might inspire you to keep striving for better achievements.

Conclusion

Measuring success in copywriting requires more than just measuring numbers. It entails comprehending what those figures signify and how they can direct your future efforts. By focussing on essential KPIs and efficiently analysing data, you can develop more engaging copy that connects with your target audience and drives results. Remember, the goal is constant development, so continue to learn and adjust based on what the data shows you.

Twelve

Continuous Improvement
The Importance of Feedback
Iterating Based on Performance

Anyone who works in copywriting must strive for continuous improvement. It entails constantly looking for ways to improve your talents and make your writing more successful.

The Importance Of Feedback

1. Gathering insights

Feedback is necessary for growth. Whether it comes from colleagues, clients, or readers, it provides essential information about how your material is perceived. It can show hidden assets as well as areas that require improvement. Asking for comments demonstrates your commitment to developing your craft.

2. Diverse perspectives.

Getting advice from others provides new perspectives. Sometimes you're too close to your work to notice its problems. A coworker may notice bad phrasing and offer a cleaner approach to explain a concept. Different perspectives can help you identify blind spots and improve your writing.

3. Promoting Collaboration.

When you request input, you are opening the door to collaboration. Working with others can generate new ideas and approaches. Engaging with other writers or marketers can inspire and help you think beyond the box. It's an opportunity to learn from one another.

4. Building Relationships

Regularly seeking feedback leads to stronger ties with clients and colleagues. When others realise that you value their feedback, they are more likely to interact with you constructively. This can lead to more fruitful collaborations and better results in initiatives.

5. Constructive criticism.

Not all feedback will be positive, and that's fine. Constructive criticism is essential for improvement. Learn to accept it instead of taking it personally. Prioritise the content over the presentation. Use this feedback to make the required modifications and advance as a writer.

6. Setting up feedback loops.

Set up a system to collect feedback on a regular basis. This could include questionnaires, one-on-one discussions, or reviews.Simplify the process for people to share their ideas. The more systematic your approach, the more likely you are to receive valuable feedback.

7. Reflecting on Feedback.

Don't only collect input; reflect on it. What patterns are you noticing? Are there any recurring suggestions? Use this insight to direct your future writing. Identify essential topics that will help lead your changes.

Iterating Based on Performance.

1. Understanding iteration.

Iteration is the process of making little modifications to better your work. It's all about experimentation, learning, and refinement. In copywriting, this is assessing your copy using performance indicators and making adjustments as appropriate.

2. Analysing Results

After gathering feedback and data, carefully analyse the results. Check for trends in your stats. For example, if one headline consistently outperforms others, try employing similar designs in future work. Recognizing what works can help you achieve success again.

3. Making Adjustments.

Based on your findings, make targeted changes to your material. This could include adjusting your headlines, improving your calls to action, or rewriting portions for clarity. Small modifications can have a significant impact on how your audience reacts.

4. Testing Changes

After making changes, test the updated version of your copy. This could be accomplished using A/B testing, in which you compare the original and changed versions. Keep track of their performances to evaluate which one resonates with your target audience the most. Testing helps to validate your modifications.

5. Learn from Failures

Not every adjustment will result in an improvement, which is a normal part of the process. If a new version does not operate as intended, investigate why. Did you overlook something in your audience's needs? Use these lessons to guide future versions.

6. Establishing Goals for Improvement

Set specific goals for each piece of copy. Having explicit objectives, whether they are to increase conversions or engagement, will help direct your revisions. To determine the effectiveness of your improvements, compare your success to these aims.

7. Keeping up with trends.

The field of copywriting is always evolving. Keep informed about industry updates and best practices. This insight can help you plan your iterations and keep ahead of the competition. To continue learning, follow relevant blogs, attend workshops, and participate in online forums.

8. Embracing a growth mindset

Adopt a growth mentality, which implies thinking that you can improve through work and practice. Consider obstacles as opportunities to learn. This approach will enable you to accept feedback and iteration as necessary components of your writing process.

9. Documenting your progress.

Keep track of your iterations and results. This documentation allows you to track your progress over time. It can also be used as a reference for future initiatives. Understanding what worked and what did not can save you time and effort in the long run.

10. Celebrating Improvements

Finally, take the time to recognise your achievements. Recognise your progress, whether through a successful campaign or great comments. Celebrating modest victories might inspire you to keep striving for better achievements.

Conclusion

Continuous improvement is an essential component of becoming a successful copywriter. You may improve your skills and write more effective copy by taking feedback seriously and iterating based on performance. Accept the process, learn from your experiences, and continually strive for improvement. The process of growth continues, and each step you take brings you closer to perfecting your craft.

Thirteen

Case Studies of Successful Copy
Analysing Effective Campaigns
Lessons Learned from Top Brands

Analysing successful copy campaigns can provide useful information about what works and why. This chapter examines successful advertisements from leading businesses and the lessons we can draw from them.

Analysing effective campaigns

1. Nike "Just Do It"

Nike's "Just Do It" motto is one of the best-known in the world. It was launched in 1988 and represents motivation and determination. Customers respond strongly to the phrase's simplicity. It sells more than simply shoes; it also sells a mindset. Nike pushes people to reach their full potential by emphasising the emotional link to sports and personal achievement.

Key Takeaway: Effective copy frequently appeals to emotions. Rather than simply promoting a product, connect with your audience's emotions and goals.

2. Apple Product Launches

Apple is well-known for its captivating product releases, particularly for the iPhone. The organisation uses simple, direct language to showcase capabilities and benefits without overwhelming customers. Their copy is straightforward but effective, eliciting excitement and expectation. Apple's marketing emphasises design and user experience, making it easy for customers to grasp why they need the latest goods.

Key Takeaway: Clarity and simplicity are essential. Avoid jargon and focus on what is most important to your readers.

3. Dove's Real Beauty Campaign.

Dove's Real Beauty campaign challenges established beauty norms. The campaign includes actual women of all shapes, sizes, and races. Dove builds a personal connection with customers by promoting self-acceptance and body positivity. This strategy promotes not only trust but also a sense of community.

Key takeaway: Authenticity is important. People value brands that are real and relatable. Highlighting real-life stories might help you build a deep connection with your audience.

4. Old Spice "The Man Your Man Could Smell Like"

Old Spice relaunched their brand with a hilarious campaign starring the character Isaiah Mustafa. The advertisements skilfully combine fun with a forceful call to action. The language is humorous and entertaining, appealing to both genders. This strategy transformed Old Spice into a cultural phenomenon, dramatically increasing sales.

Key Takeaway: Humour may be an effective weapon. When used appropriately, it may help your message become memorable and shared.

5. Airbnb: "Belong Anywhere"

Airbnb "Belong Anywhere" and emphasises the feeling of belonging and connection. The copy focusses on experiences rather than merely accommodations. Airbnb builds an emotional connection with its audience by relaying the tales of guests and hosts. This tactic helped to promote Airbnb as more than just a place to stay; it is about community and belonging.

Key Takeaway: Concentrate on experiences. People are drawn to stories that relate with their own experiences and goals.

Lessons from Top Brands

1. Know Your Audience

All great initiatives begin with a thorough understanding of their target audience. Brands such as Nike and Dove invest substantially in market research to better understand their customers' wants and preferences. Tailoring your message to your target audience's tastes boosts the likelihood of engagement and conversion.

2. Develop a strong brand voice.

A consistent brand voice promotes recognition and trust. Apple's clean and modern tone, for example, is consistent with its product design and target clientele. Establishing a clear voice means that your entire writing reflects your brand identity, making it more memorable.

3. Use Storytelling.

Storytelling is an effective approach to communicate with your audience. Dove and Airbnb leverage human storytelling in their campaigns. When people identify with a narrative, they are more likely to remember it and share it with others.

4. Concentrate on benefits, not features.

While features are crucial, buyers are more concerned about how a product will benefit their life. Apple's marketing frequently emphasises how their goods improve user experience rather than simply stating technical characteristics. Always frame your material to highlight the benefits for the customer.

5. Encourage Engagement

Old Spice's ad invited viewers to engage by responding to social media comments. This type of involvement promotes a sense of community and loyalty. When individuals feel engaged, they are more likely to spread your message and become brand ambassadors.

6. Test and iterate.

Top brands often test their language and campaigns to see what works best. They review performance data and make changes based on what resonates with their target audience. Learning from both achievements and mistakes is critical for continual improvement.

7. Emphasise emotional appeal.

Emotional connections influence consumer behaviour. Nike's and Dove's campaigns appeal to aspiration, confidence, and acceptance. When your text elicits emotions, it becomes more effective and remembered.

8. Keep it simple.

Avoid filling your copy with unnecessary material. Effective advertisements, such as Apple's, emphasise clear, simple statements that highlight essential features. Simplicity helps people grasp and act on your message.

9. Be authentic.

Authenticity promotes trust. Consumers may detect whether a brand is being deceptive. Dove succeeds because it delivers a genuine message that resonates with its audience. Stay true to your brand's principles and speak openly.

10. Monitor trends and adapt

Successful brands pay close attention to market developments and adjust their tactics accordingly. This flexibility enables them to remain relevant and fulfil changing consumer demands. Be open to changing your copy and approach based on comments and new insights.

Conclusion

Studying successful copy campaigns teaches copywriters crucial things. You may improve your writing by studying what works and learning from great brands' techniques. Remember to concentrate on your audience, deliver fascinating stories, and be real. Each campaign provides insights that will help you write more effective and interesting copy in the future. Accept these lessons and always change your approach to stay competitive in the ever-changing world of copywriting.

Fourteen

Final Thoughts and Next Steps
Building a Copywriting Strategy
Resources for Further Learning

As you progress in your copywriting career, it's critical to focus on developing a strong approach and knowing where to acquire additional resources. Here's how you may take specific actions to improve your copywriting skills and efficacy.

Creating a Copywriting Strategy

Define your goals.

Begin by clearly identifying your copywriting goals. Are you looking to improve sales, internet traffic, or cultivate a loyal following? Setting specific goals will help you write focused and effective copy. Write down your goals so you can refer to them while you work.

Understand your audience.

Knowing your audience is critical for creating good copy. Create thorough profiles for your ideal customers, including their age, interests, and pain areas. Conduct surveys or use social media to collect data. The better you know your target audience, the more relevant your copy will be.

Create a unique brand voice.

Your brand voice represents the way you interact with your target audience. Choose a tone that expresses your brand's individuality. Whether it's friendly, professional, or quirky, consistency is essential. This helps people recognise and connect with your brand, making it more memorable.

Create a content calendar.

Use a content calendar to organise your writing. Plan your subjects, formats, and posting schedule in advance. This not only keeps you on schedule, but also assures a consistent flow of information. Include key dates, campaigns, and themes to help guide your writing.

Create Strong Headlines

Headlines are the first thing people see, so make them memorable. An excellent headline captures the reader's attention and urges them to continue. Make them more intriguing by using figures, questions, or power words. Spend time creating headlines that effectively express the importance of your material.

Highlight Benefits Over Features.

When presenting a product or service, emphasise the benefits rather than the features. Explain how your offering addresses problems or enhances people's lives. This method connects better with readers and helps them recognise the value in what you're delivering.

Include clear calls to action.

Every piece of writing should tell readers what to do next. A clear call to action (CTA) tells people what you want them to do, whether it's subscribe to a newsletter, make a purchase, or share your content. Make your CTAs clear and enticing.

Test and adapt.

Testing is vital for determining what works best. Utilise A/B testing to evaluate different versions of your content. Analyse performance data to determine which headlines, CTAs, and styles work best. Use this information to prove your copy and future promotions.

Gather Feedback.

Seek input from your peers or audience. Constructive criticism can pinpoint areas where you can improve. Regularly assess your work and be willing to make modifications. This will help you improve as a writer and connect with your readers.

Maintain consistency.

Consistency in messaging and branding fosters trust. Make sure all of your copy is consistent with your brand's values and voice. This gives your viewers a consistent experience, boosting their chances of connecting with your material.

Resources for Further Learning

Books

Reading can improve your comprehension of copywriting. Look for titles that cover compelling writing, effective narrative, and marketing principles. Concentrate on publications that provide practical exercises and real-world examples for applying topics in your workplace. Interacting with people from different backgrounds helps you improve your talents and expand your ideas.

Online Courses

Think about enrolling in an online course to enhance your skills. Some preferred platforms are:

-**Coursera:** University and industry specialists teach courses on various topics of writing and marketing.
- **Udemy**: Offers a variety of affordable courses on copywriting skills.
- **Skillshare:** Offers brief classes given by skilled writers and marketers that tackle practical topics.

www.ingramcontent.com/pod-product-compliance
Lightning Source LLC
Chambersburg PA
CBHW071943210526
45479CB00002B/790